This book belongs to

_____

Paperback ISBN: 978-1-63731-530-9
Hardcover ISBN: 978-1-63731-532-3

Hooty Pooty
the
Owl

By Humor
Heals Us

Hooty Pooty is a farting owl.
He can't help his stinky bowel.
Most owls cry "Hoot, hoot, hoot!"
But Hooty Pooty cries, "Poot, poot, poot!"

There are owls of many kinds,
And I know that may be fine.
But as soon as the hooting starts
Hooty Pooty releases stinky farts.

Owls hunt for food during the night,
So that's when they all take to flight.
And Hooty Pooty flies extremely fast
For he has an extra special blast!

A barn provides a place to rest,
For easy prey, it's the best.
Hooty Pooty sits high without a sound,
Waiting for movement to swoop down.

Mice and rats will quickly scatter,
Although it really doesn't matter.
Hooty Pooty flies down with a zoom,
Sounding like a sonic boom.

When he's perched in a tall tree
Hooty Pooty lets his farts fly free.
Other birds don't like the smell
But Hooty Pooty thinks his scent is swell.

The other owls all seem too serious,
But maybe they are all just envious.
For Hooty Pooty farts without a care,
And catches lots of food to share.

The animals all run and hide -
No one is on poor Hooty Pooty's side.
When he tries to make new friends
Because he farts, all his friendships end.

He flaps his wings and gives a hoot,
But suddenly lets out a "poot!"
The other owls then cough and sputter
And fly away with great flutter.

But one fine day in mid-July
An eagle hovered in the sky.
The nests were full of young owl chicks,
They tried to hide among the sticks.

But eagles have very sharp eyes.
It saw the chicks, oooh a yummy prize!
It circled wide and then it swooped.
The owls all huddled in a group.

They tried their best
To protect their nests.
Owls are wise, as we all know,
But eagles are a mighty foe.

Hooty Pooty knew he had to act.
He has a weapon, that's a fact.
He lifted his tail to the sky -
A massive stinky fart, he let fly.

The eagle's plunge came to a stop,
And then it dropped like it was shot.
Hooty Pooty's fart bomb hit the eagle in the head,
It began twirling near the shed.

The eagle fell hard to the ground.
It just lay there and made no sound.
Hooty Pooty poked it with his beak.
It was alive but very weak.

He said, "You're free to fly away,
But when you're home there you must stay.
Never come back here again,
That fart was just eight out of ten."

The eagle stood up, spread it's wings.
And said, "You're the farting king.
Your farts are powerful and they stink.
I'll stay away from you, I think."

It flew away and never returned,
All the eagles appreciated the lesson learned.
They must not judge and instead accept.
From then on, Hooty Pooty gained respect.

He had become the king of owls,
For he could hoot, and poot, and howl.
If predators ever attacked,
King Hooty Pooty's farts would turn them back.

Follow us on FB and IG @humorhealsus
To vote on new title names and freebies, visit
us at humorhealsus.com for more information.

@humorhealsus   @humorhealsus

www.ingramcontent.com/pod-product-compliance
Lightning Source LLC
Chambersburg PA
CBHW042024090426

42811CB00016B/1735